BRIEF VISITS

SONNETS FROM A VOLUNTEER CHAPLAIN

BRIEF VISITS

SONNETS FROM A VOLUNTEER CHAPLAIN

Susan Palwick

Texas Review Press
Huntsville, Texas

FIRST EDITION, 2012
Requests for permission to reproduce material from this work should be
sent to:

Permissions
Texas Review Press
English Department
Sam Houston State University
Huntsville, TX 77341-2146

Acknowledgements:

Author photo courtesy of Eugene Ghymn
Cover design by Nancy Parsons, Graphic Design Group

Library of Congress Cataloging-in-Publication Data

Library of Congress Cataloging-in-Publication Data
Palwick, Susan.
Brief visits : sonnets from a volunteer chaplain / Susan Palwick.
p. cm.
ISBN 978-1-933896-88-5 (pbk. : alk. paper)
1. Hospitals—Emergency services—Poetry. I. Title.
PS3566.A554B75 2012
811'.54—dc23
2012024371

For Sherry Dunn,
who taught me what a chaplain looks like,
and for Doris L. Meyer,
a model of kindness and courage

CONTENTS

Preface: So Many Syllables

In October 2004, I began volunteering as a lay chaplain in the emergency room of a local hospital. At the time, I was in process to be ordained as a deacon in the Episcopal Church, which required pastoral-care experience. Accordingly, I enrolled in a seven-month Clinical Pastoral Education (CPE) program—intensive chaplaincy training—at a local hospital.

It was the wrong time for me to undertake that grueling a program, and I withdrew after two months. (I also eventually withdrew from ordination, although I am still a licensed lay preacher in the Episcopal Diocese of Nevada.) I learned, though, that I love working in the ER, which offers the greatest variety of any department in the hospital: patients of all ages, outlooks and conditions, from every possible walk of life. To me, the ER is one incarnation of the Body of Christ. It doesn't hurt that I've always been fascinated by medicine and am, in a modest way, an adrenaline junkie. It also doesn't hurt that I have a reasonably strong stomach. My hospital isn't a trauma center, but the sights, sounds and smells of the ER can still be unsettling.

Sadly, my hospital was recently sold, and the new owners promptly closed the Spiritual Care Department. Without staff chaplains to supervise volunteers, the volunteer-chaplaincy program was discontinued. I cannot overstate the loss this represents to hospital patients and staff. Spirituality – the process of finding and making larger meanings – is especially important to people who are ill or injured, even if they are not religious in any conventional sense. Hospital patients hang above voids and chasms, and have long hours to contemplate those dark spaces, and are often afraid or in pain. Chaplains can help them navigate this strange territory. But there is no billing code for spiritual care, and in today's healthcare environment, what cannot be billed all too often must be acquired elsewhere.

In many hospitals, I wouldn't even have been allowed to call myself a chaplain. Pastoral care in healthcare settings is increasingly provided by board-certified chaplains: clergy with divinity degrees, 1,600 hours of CPE, and at least 1,000 hours of professional experience. The hospital where I volunteered, however—which I have been advised not to name, lest anyone believe I am speaking for the institution—trained laypeople to provide spiritual care. When I withdrew from CPE, the volunteer-chaplaincy supervisor decided that my brief stint in the program was more than equivalent to volunteer training, and allowed me to continue in that role.

Because my hospital ID badge read "volunteer chaplain," that is what I called myself. Some people with the same ID badge told patients, "I'm a volunteer from the Spiritual Care Department." Whenever I tried saying that, though, the patient stared at me in bewilderment.

"You're a *what*?"

Sick people can only deal with so many syllables.

So I stuck with "volunteer chaplain," and became a passionate advocate for both the role and its title. Listening to, and praying with, ill and worried people doesn't require advanced degrees and thousands of hours of training. It does require compassion, an open mind, sensitivity to a range of spiritual traditions and approaches—I was trained to minister to patients of any religious faith, or none—and a willingness to be present to pain of all kinds.

The work done by volunteers at my hospital helped free the staff chaplains, the board-certified professionals, for complicated cases that only they could handle. The professional chaplains knew more about the vast spectrum of human spiritual traditions than I did. They had more experience with thorny ethical situations than I did. As clergy, they could perform sacramental functions I could not. But the reverse was also true: I could help patients in some ways the professionals couldn't.

Vulnerability is one of the biggest taboos in American culture. We live in a society that values competence, strength, and independence. Hospital patients, vulnerable and dependent by definition, often feel deeply ashamed of their human frailty. Patients have apologized to me for crying, for bleeding, for being smelly or frightened.

In my religious tradition, grace is defined as a free, unearned gift from God. When patients learned that I was a volunteer, their eyes often widened in wonder. I had come to be with them in all their human vulnerability, even if—or especially when—they were smelly, bleeding, and frightened. I had arrived at their bedside, offering conversation and prayer and warm blankets, *even though I wasn't being paid for it.* As a volunteer, I modeled divine grace in ways that professional staff, by simple virtue of their hard-earned paychecks, could not.

At the end of my last shift in May 2012, I had worked 1,132 hours in the ER. (In the hospital, it's known as the Emergency Department or ED, rather than ER, but I've used the more popular and recognizable term here.) Although I took breaks from the work—notably a leave of many months while my father was dying—I always came back to it. I worked four hours a week, either in one long shift or two shorter ones, depending on my schedule. During each shift, I tried to visit every patient in the department. Medical staff sometimes asked me to visit especially anxious patients, patients who had just received a devastating diagnosis, or the loved ones of patients who had died. I quickly learned, though, that many of the most profound spiritual needs weren't visible to medical staff. Patients will tell a chaplain things they won't tell a nurse or doctor, and someone with a minor injury may be navigating a major loss.

Because I am also a writer and English professor, the narrative aspects of the work—medical crisis as story—fascinated me from the beginning. Through my ER ministry, I became very interested in Narrative Medicine (NM), a field pioneered by Dr.

Rita Charon at Columbia University Hospital of Physicians and Surgeons in New York. Charon uses basic literary theory to train medical providers to be more careful listeners to patient stories, which makes them better providers. I took her introductory NM workshop during the summer of 2009, and now teach NM as adjunct faculty at the University of Nevada School of Medicine.

Patients own their own stories, but the story of what a volunteer shift feels like—its rhythms and tensions, the emotions it elicits—is the volunteer's. Although I write primarily prose fiction, I have always found it easiest to describe my hospital work in poetry, partly because chaplaincy visits are usually very short, a few minutes at most. "Ours is a brief ministry," we were taught in training.

One day three or four years ago, it occurred to me that a sonnet sequence might be an excellent way to capture the feeling of my hospital work. This chapbook is the result. Like a sonnet, a chaplaincy visit is highly structured and circumscribed. A sonnet has only 140 syllables; at the bedside, I had time for only so many syllables of greeting and comfort. Because chaplains do more listening than talking, most of the syllables uttered during a visit are the patient's, and I have written these sonnets accordingly, often using voices other than my own.

Patients own their own stories. These poems are fiction: while all are based on visits with actual patients, I have changed identifying details, have included no names, and have used an ER floorplan that no longer exists. The sonnets tell the story of a complete shift, with roughly one sonnet per visit. I never had a single shift that contained this much drama, but I could have, had the timing been a little different: nothing here is outside the boundaries of an ordinary day in the department.

While the hospital always had a staff chaplain on call, ready to come in on short notice, I was occasionally the only chaplain of any sort in the building. I have set this narrative during one such time. In the absence of staff chaplains, I was instructed to respond to Code Blues elsewhere in the hospital, a situation I write about here.

While I fear this preface already contains too many syllables, I wish to close with acknowledgments. This chapbook was made possible by the communities in which I live and work: by everyone, patients and staff and fellow volunteers, at my hospital; by the people of St. Stephen's Episcopal Church in Reno and St. Paul's Episcopal Church in Sparks; by my friends in the Department of English and the School of Medicine at the University of Nevada, Reno. I am especially grateful to UNR for the boon of a professional development leave from my university teaching duties, during which I finished this project, and for support from the Scholarly and Creative Activities Grants Program of the College of Liberal Arts.

For specific feedback about this manuscript, I am particularly indebted to my colleague Ann Keniston, a gracious and greatly gifted poet; to my husband Gary Meyer, who reads everything

I do and always helps me make it better, and to Paul Ruffin at Texas Review Press, who offered to publish these poems. Many, many more of you (including early readers of individual sonnets posted on my blog) must remain nameless. There are not enough syllables to express my gratitude, but here are two: Thank you.

Susan Palwick
Pentecost 2012
Reno, Nevada

BRIEF VISITS

SONNETS FROM A VOLUNTEER CHAPLAIN

SETTING OUT

Preparing has become a ritual:
I iron cotton scrubs—the cheerful clothes
I always wear—and as each wrinkle goes,
I pray, petitions so habitual
I rarely put them into words. *Help me*
help others smooth the creases of their lives;
grant me the grace to summon what revives
each soul, the steam that freshens. Keep me free
from scorching blunders. Now the dinner, quick
and healthy, that my husband has prepared.
Brush teeth. Wash hands. Rebuke unruly hair.
Calm stomach when it does a flutter kick.
Hug Gary when he looks into my eyes
and says, "Good luck. I hope nobody dies."

SIGNING IN

First stop's the chaplains' office, a small space
with sink and closet, sign-in book, and shelves
piled high with treats for patients, and ourselves:
tissues and crayons (vehicles of grace),
ten kinds of prayer cards, plastic rosaries—
bright presents, made by other volunteers—
a stack of Bibles. This is where my fears
intensify, the panicky unease
about what's waiting for me. Never mind.
I'll find out when I get there. Here's the slip
of paper that will purchase a small snack
if, later, I need sugar to unwind,
kill time, or celebrate. And now the trip
downstairs. Breathe. In four hours, I'll be back.

EMERGENCY TRAUMA FAMILY CONSULT ROOM

This hallway leading to Emergency
goes on forever, free (this time of night)
of patients, but I look ahead and see
an open door—*that* room—the spill of light,
and now I hear soft sobbing, step inside,
say, "I'm the chaplain; can I help you?" "Yes,
you can, dear." Resolute and dignified,
she tells me that the doctors cannot guess
her husband's outcome, if he'll even live.
"It's bad," she says. I know. This room is where
we send them when it's bad. "I'll check, and give
you any news I learn," I promise her.
We pray and hug. She's tear-wracked and adrift.
This is the worst way to begin a shift.

ROOM 2

The code room's chaos, even if contained,
a sea of feet beneath the curtain drawn
for privacy. The staff stay calm. They're trained
for this. (At least here: I remember one
nurse on another floor who said, "I can't
deal with the drama. Codes just aren't my thing.")
I wait and watch outside, bide time—don't want
to be a pest—pray for encouraging
news for the wife, if any's to be had.
And here's the doc, a nice one, purposeful
but kind. "What news?" She grimaces. It's bad,
I think, but then she says, "He's critical,
but stable. Vitals good." "Good! May I tell
his wife?" "Of course." For now, we've side-stepped hell.

ER SIGN-IN

The wife's incredibly relieved. I muse
on how this place destroys all everyday
proportion, old perspectives swept away,
"he's on a ventilator" better news
than "nothing worked," both fates you'd never choose.
The choices here are grim, the least delay
of death a gift. The wife says, "No, don't stay;
so many others need you." That's a ruse
we often hear, polite dismissal, but
she means it. Late, I sign the ER board
in marker: "Chaplain: Susan, 5 to 9."
The charge nurse says, "We've got a kid who cut
herself. The mom's got problems too." "Oh, Lord,"
a medic groans. I'm on it; this one's mine.

HALL BED 5

I'm on it; this one's mine. They're in the hall,
which means the rooms are full. As I approach
I hear the mother hissing, "After all
I've done for you!" *A fine time for reproach.*
"I wish I'd never had you!" *Charming, Mom.*
Her suit drips wealth. The daughter smiles at me,
chides gently, "Mom, that's mean." Is she this calm
at home? And where the hell's security?
I introduce myself. "Ma'am, you're upset,
but this won't help. Perhaps you need to go
and cool off in the waiting room?" I get
a glare, crossed arms. "I won't!" She quiets, though.
The girl, wrists bleeding, says, "It's nice of you
to visit." Who's the saner of these two?

ROOM 8

The doctor comes; I leave. A patient waves
me down across the hall. "Why can't you throw
her out? I wouldn't want a dog to go
through that! Poor kid! The way that mom behaves,
she shouldn't have a child! The woman's nuts!"
So much for HIPAA. "Listen, I agree,
but I don't have that much authority;
I'm just a volunteer." I gently shut
the door. "That's hard to hear when you're in pain
yourself. I'm sorry." "Oh, I'm fine. It's just
a boil. I hope the girl will be all right."
"I hope so too," I say, but don't explain
the three-day psych hold, which in this case must
seem like vacation. Was the cutting flight?

ROOM 1

Bed 1.1

Right now I feel less holy than a head
of cabbage. It's too early for a break—
I've only seen three patients—so instead
I'll choose an easy room (I hope) to make
this stretch less draining. Ah, one-one's asleep;
that worked out well. He's middle-aged and gaunt,
cheeks sunken, forehead bloody, clothes a heap
beside the bed. He twitches. Spirits haunt
his dreams: distilled, I think. Oblivious
to wailing from next door, he snores in peace,
hands pillowing his cheek. I'm envious.
I practice seeing Christ in him, release
my anger at the mom, note irony.
Yes, when they're sleeping, love comes easily.

Bed 1.2

Next door, a baby howls. His parents—young
and anxious—hover, cuddle, whisper rhymes
and lullabies. "He's gorgeous, with the lungs
of champions," I say. They laugh. "Each time
he's sick, we get so scared! We hate to bring
him here, but with this fever . . .Tylenol's
no good. The doctors want to do this thing—
a spinal tap?" The baby caterwauls
so loudly I can hardly hear them. Then
a doctor, nurse and EMT arrive:
time for the test. "I'll come and visit when
they're done," I say. The baby will survive
this better than his parents, I've no doubt.
They haven't heard. The doctor's in; I'm out.

Bed 1.3

"Hello! Aren't you a sweetheart to come by!"
She's sitting up and beaming, ankle propped
on pillows. "I sure hope that little guy
will be all right." (Have curtains ever stopped
the slightest sound? Is HIPAA unaware
that cotton's not concrete?) "That foot looks sore,"
I say. She nods. "I tumbled down the stairs.
The puppy tripped me. Now we're waiting for
the films. They think I might need surgery."
"That's awful! Did the pup apologize?"
She chortles. "Duke's a big old baby, see,
a Newfoundland who doesn't know his size.
My son's home walking him—oh, here's my nurse!
Thanks, Susan: pray this evening gets no worse!"

ROOM 3

Bed 3.1

Her hair's a tangled mass, spun fine and white
—bird's nest or halo—soft and disarrayed.
She's bird-thin, too, and like a bird, afraid
of sudden noise, new people. "It's all right,"
I tell her. "I'm the chaplain. Do you need
a tissue?" She's begun to weep. I find
a Kleenex, wipe her face. They've had to bind
her to the bed: dementia. Were she freed,
she'd wander, but she's no less lost with us.
"Her husband dumped her here," the nurse explains.
Head cocked, the patient peers at me and strains
against the bonds. Her eyes are luminous,
pale blue. She speaks now. "Mama?" That faint cry
grows louder, so I sing a lullaby.

Bed 3.2

He's hooked to leads, blood pressure monitor,
IVs: a maze of tubes. "My three kids died
last year: a car crash. I've been crucified,
you know? I can't tell what I'm living for.
My wife, I guess. Each day's a funeral
at our house. Now I need heart surgery."
I squeeze his hand. "That kind of tragedy
would flatten anyone." *Original!*
Just what he needs: clichés. "What helps you get
up every day?" "My faith. This agony's
God's gift to make me grateful they're not here,
where so much hurts." I blink. My eyes are wet.
We're trained to deal with bad theology:
It's theirs. They need it. Do not interfere.

Bed 3.3

He glares at me the moment I appear.
"So you're the chaplain? Lady, I've no use
for your profession." *What, you've been abused
by English teachers?* "That's okay. I'm here
to offer any help I can: some talk
to pass the time, a blanket?" "Yeah, you'll plot
to get me into church! No thanks. I've got
more sense than that." I smile and start to walk
away: I don't get paid enough to deal
with insults. "Hey! So what makes you believe?"
I turn. "That's isn't anything I can
explain with formulas. My faith is real
but complicated." Now he looks relieved.
"It's hogwash even you don't understand!"

CHAPEL I

It's almost always empty when I come;
I'm almost always empty, which is why
I come. I sit. I breathe. I notice some-
one else, off in a corner, and I try
to let myself be filled. I cannot bring
God's love to others if I do not feel
that love myself. I don't feel anything
right now except exhaustion. Should I kneel?
No: I'm too tired. Sit and pray. *Dear God,*
make me your hands, your feet, a hollow reed
through which you speak. Make me your lightning rod,
your vessel. Help me give them what they need.
Has that done anything? I'll only know
by visiting more patients. Time to go.

HALL BED 1

They've brought her in on CareFlight: broken hip.
She's eighty-eight, four hours from her home
by car, and no one's with her. "I'm alone,"
she says. "Oh, I have neighbors, but this trip's
too long for them. Please, sweetheart, will you pray
with me? The Lord's Prayer, maybe? That would make
me happy. Jesus bless you, dear!" I take
her chilly hand in mine. We start to say
the prayer. *Our Father . . . .* When we reach *forgive*,
she says *trespasses.* I say *sins.* Her eyes
fly open. "You just changed God's Holy Word!
That's unforgivable!" I bite my cheek
to keep from laughing. "Ma'am, you realize
they're both translations?" Icy, undeterred,
she glares. I might as well be speaking Greek.

HALL BED 3

A homeless guy arrives by ambulance.
"ETOH on board," the medic says,
and rolls his eyes. The nurse is even less
amused. "Stop cursing!"—giving me a glance—
"This woman is our chaplain! Be polite!"
The patient, halfway through a graceful stream
of expletives, sits up and grins. "You seem
to be a lady, chaplain! Well, all right.
You pray?" "Of course." He beams at me. "Me too!
Most every morning: 'Hey there, Big Dude!' Then
God answers: 'Hey there, little dude!' And when
I've fed the birds, well, me and God, we chew
the fat a while. He feeds me like a bird."
I laugh, delighted. This one has the Word.

ROOM 4

Bed 4.1

I hear the rhythmic hissing of the vent
before I see the bed. "She shouldn't have
been intubated. Nothing curative
will come of this," the nurse says. "If she'd meant
to be on life support, there wouldn't be
a DNR! The nursing home misplaced
the file, and then they panicked when they faced
the code, called 911. Her family
has tough decisions now. I hate this stuff!"
I look down at the patient, pale and still,
so like a corpse already. Were that hiss
of air God's voice, would I still hear, "Enough?"
The son arrives—*Lord, help us do your will*—
and chokes, "She wouldn't want to be like this."

Bed 4.2

"My husband left me when I had the stroke
last year. He couldn't stand to see me sick.
He's not a bad man, really, but it broke
my heart to see him go. We'd been through thick
and thin for fourteen years. Oh, God, I miss
him more each morning! Will you help me pray?
Our baby's only two, and I'm on dis-
ability. I don't know how I'll pay
the bills. My daughter's such an angel: she's
what keeps me going. Please, let's pray." We do.
We pray for comfort, strength, security.
I pray that she'll find someone loving, who
won't flee mortality, won't disavow
"in sickness." But I don't say that aloud.

Bed 4.3

And here we have a Brady Bunch, or three:
the patient, wife and son, son's wife, their tot,
an older child. They all sit quietly,
which must be why the loyal tribe has not
been asked to leave. They don't want prayer, but ask
if dad can have a blanket, if the son
can have some water. Glad for simple tasks,
I cheerfully take all requests, and run
all errands: crayons for the little boy,
a plush toy for the baby ("you can take
that home"). Such simple service! I enjoy
the specificity, how crayons make
grace visible. I steel myself for codes,
but always welcome flight-attendant mode.

ROOM 5

Bed 5.1

Room five's for criticals, and has four beds.
The only room that's scarier is 2,
though many patients here go home instead
of being brought upstairs, to ICU.
This corner's where I first saw someone dead.
We'd prayed; her voice had vanished, but I knew
from her expression what she would have said
could she have spoken: "Help me. Help me! Do
you understand?" (A dying cat once stared
at me like that.) I held her hands and prayed;
she struggled less. But later when I went
to check on her, the patient wasn't there:
a cold corpse lay, eyes open and afraid,
fixed face a mute mask of abandonment.

Bed 5.2

The patient smiles. "Do you believe in ghosts?"
I nod, try not to grimace; in this room
my ghosts do somersaults, and spreading gloom's
not what I'm paid—unpaid!—for. (It's almost
a year since that old lady died, and still
Bed One unnerves me. That's why I'm relieved
no patient's there right now.) "Then you'll believe
this story. When my dearest friend fell ill,
I drove to see her, but before I'd hit
the halfway point, I felt her singing soul
blow through me like a mist, and knew she'd passed.
But oh, that tune was joyous! Hearing it,
I knew that she was happy, well, and whole.
I hum it now for healing, and hold fast."

Bed 5.3

His skin's fine parchment, yellowed, leathery.
A woman at the bedside weeps. "I'm not
his daughter, no. If he has family,
I've never seen them! Listen, there's a lot
I'd tell them if I could! I'm just an aide:
I empty bedpans at the nursing home.
But this old guy—he's failing. I'm afraid
he's dying, and I love him like my own.
That doesn't happen often: maybe twice
in fifteen years I've felt this way about
a resident. I know the best advice
is not to get involved. Don't care. Stay out
of other people's lives—but how could I
stand knowing he'd come here, alone, to die?"

Bed 5.4

"I've had ten heart attacks, three surgeries,
more Cath Lab visits than I care to count.
Tonight they want me in telemetry.
I shudder when I think of the amount
of rent I've paid here! But, you know, each day's
a gift. That near-death thing? Been there, done that.
Three times—although I never saw that blaze
of light they talk about, just darkness. What
a darkness! Soft as velvet, warm as skin,
pure peace. The strongest drugs they have can't touch
that feeling. Maybe it's like being in
the womb; I wouldn't know. But there's not much
that scares me now. Death doesn't, anyway.
I wish they'd hurry with my dinner tray!"

BREAK

I need a snack. I head to the canteen,
but glance at beds along the way. Room 2
is empty—he must be in ICU—
and in 1.2, the baby's gone, bed clean.
I guess the spinal tap was negative;
that calls for treats. My four-buck coupon buys
one fresh-baked cookie, water (smallish size),
and a banana. Here's a relative,
one of the 4.3 clan; we smile and nod.
I sit and munch, and think how every shift
the patients give me far more than they get.
Those tales in 5 were bulletins from God:
surprising, ghost-assuaging grace, the gift
of postcards from a place I don't know yet.

HALL BED 6

He's been asleep, but as I pass, he stirs:
squints up at me, and when I introduce
myself—"I visit everyone, in case
they need to talk"—he nods. "I need to talk
about how no one understands. It's worse
when doctors don't; they should. There's some excuse
for other people. No one knows!" His face
begins to crumple. Techs and nurses walk
obliviously past. "What would you tell
us if you could?" He shivers. "What it's like
to hear the voices." "I don't understand
that either, but I really want to. Will
you tell me?" "Sure." He almost smiles—for psych
evals, that's huge—and reaches for my hand.

ROOM 6.1

But first, I ask his nurse if we can move
him to a newly empty room. "I hate
this hallway; everybody stares!" The nurse
agrees. He tells me how for twenty years
three ceaseless voices have harangued him, have
not once been silenced, can't be medicat-
ed into stillness, only grow perverse-
ly louder when he sleeps, won't disappear
until he's gone himself. "They want me dead."
He has a job. He had a family,
but they walked out two weeks ago. The din's
excruciating: "Die!" He's here instead.
I praise his strength; he nods distractedly.
I'd surely, in his place, have given in.

ROOM 6.2

The door's closed, which could mean that an exam
is underway, or that the patient wants
to sleep. I knock and hear a faint response:
"Come in," not "go away." Inside, the man
upon the bed is skeletal, and when
I say that I'm the chaplain, he begins
to weep. "I visit everybody in
the ER; don't be scared!" He smiles, extends
his hand. "I'm not. I'm dying—HIV—
and just a little while ago I prayed
for God to show me that he loves me, for
a sign. And then you came. You're proof that he
still listens. I don't have to be afraid;
I know I'm not an outcast anymore."

ROOM 7

"We're here on holiday." The husband's wan.
They're Swedish, twenty-five-ish, tall and fair;
he sits beside the bed and strokes her hair.
"We'd just learned I was pregnant: now it's gone,
the baby." She seems calmer than her mate,
although that may be shock. "It's very sad:
so strange to lose this child we barely had."
Her voice is dreamy, slurred: they've medicat-
ed her for pain, no doubt. "We'll try again,"
her husband says. She reaches up to kiss
his hand. I tell them, "Recognize your grief
and honor it: make room for mourning when
you feel the need. Some people will dismiss
this loss. It's real, despite their disbelief."

ROOM 9

He's handcuffed to a gurney, with two guards
outside: corrections officers. I ask
if I can talk to him. They gesture towards
the bed and shrug. "Proceed at your own risk."
But they're more bored than wary: it's a dare
to spook the female chaplain. (CYA
pertains as well, no doubt.) I feel their stares
inside the room. Their charge sends me away,
politely. Inmates almost always do:
the lack of privacy, I think. Outside,
the med staff gossips. "What's he in for? What's
his sentence? Is he faking?" But a few
are somber. "Look, it's stomach cancer. Hide
the smirks, okay? He'll die. No faking that."

ROOM 10

Chair 10.1

This room has dental chairs instead of beds,
and houses ear infections, injured eyes,
cat scratches, nosebleeds, rashes, boils and hives.
Why are these patients here, I think, instead
of Fast Track? Take this guy, who burned his hands
and needs the dressings changed: emergency?
I'm puzzled, but we banter pleasantly
about his job, the weather, foreign lands
he's visited. And then in that same tone—
relaxed and casual—he tells me how
the devil lives inside his radio,
prefers rock stations, won't leave him alone,
drowns out his favorite songs. "I had to buy
an iPod. He's not there yet, but he'll try."

Chair 10.2

And here we have a mom and little boy,
wide-eyed at what they've heard. *HIPAA, hurray!*
I smile to reassure them. They can't say
a word Chair One won't hear. "Do you *enjoy*
this job?" the mother asks. "Oh, yes!" Her code
is clear: You like to talk to folks like that?
I really do: the universe is vast,
exhilarating. These small rooms bestow
huge gifts, God's strangeness shining from each tale,
particular and poignant. "So what brings
you here tonight?" The child looks up, looks sad.
"Sam bit me. He's my dog. He was on sale,
but now we have to take him back." He clings
to Mom. "He wasn't trying to be bad!"

CODE

It comes through on the overhead: "Code Blue,
Room 557." Every chaplain in
the building goes to codes, but I'm alone
tonight, the cavalry. *That's ICU.*
I take the elevator with the team
from the ER. Nobody runs, except
on TV shows. I know what to expect:
the swarm of staff, equipment, feet, the same
crazed scene I saw downstairs. I wait outside,
nerves taut. *He must have gone to ICU.*
Please, please be someone else. As if on cue,
a nurse says, "In the lounge—his wife's beside
herself—could you—" "Of course." In here I'm just
a nuisance. *Please be someone else. She must.*

ICU WAITING ROOM

She's not. She's pacing. "You again! You get
around this place!" She tries to laugh. She can't.
I swallow. "I'm so sorry. Do you want
me here?" "Of course. Have they —" "No news as yet."
I speak too quickly. No news isn't good.
She shakes her head. "I don't know how to pray
right now. Downstairs, I knew just what to say:
let him survive. It worked; God understood.
But now I'm here again. I can't go through
this anymore!" "We pray God's will be done,"
I tell her sadly, "maybe most when we
don't know our own." "It's always done." "That's true;
we pray for acc—" "Oh, God, the doctor's come!"
He clears his throat; his voice cracks anyway.

CHAPEL II

She didn't want me there. Downstairs, she clung
to courtesy, but God reneged, and I'm
God's representative, who couldn't climb
up far enough to reach him, whose thick tongue
could form no pleading powerful enough
to ward off death. *Let us accept your will,*
acknowledging that every Lazarus
must die again at last. It's obvious:
all miracles are temporary till
the final Easter. Help us persevere
through our most dreadful Fridays. Let us trust
in resurrection. Comfort us in pain.
I kneel—most hollow reed—and pray, and hear
an echo: *Ash to ashes, dust to dust.*
Not news. Get up: best get to work again.

ROOM 11

Bed 11.1

"We're visiting from Iowa," she says.
"We're flying back tomorrow, if we can.
We had a lovely time, until we stuffed
ourselves at the buffet: oh, what a sight!
Roast beef, asparagus with hollandaise,
shrimp cocktail, pasta . . . " *All in warming pans,*
I think, *and incubating germs as tough
as rubber chicken.* "We were up all night,"
she says. "It all gushed out from either end.
And now we're terrified we'll miss our flight
back home. I could reschedule, but my friend's
less flexible." "I'm sure you'll be all right,"
I say. "They'll give you fluids, and you'll mend
in no time." *Welcome to Casino Blight.*

Bed 11.2

And here's her friend, still green, the Tweedledee
to Bed One's Tweedledum. "I have to be
in Iowa! My nephew's getting back
this Wednesday. He was injured in Iraq;
he lost a leg, and heaven only knows
about his head. I'm scared. My sister goes
to a support group—soldiers' relatives—
but I can't stand it. What he's suffered gives
me nightmares. I'm on medication now:
anxiety. We thought this Reno trip
might be a fun distraction, a release.
It hasn't helped. I can't imagine how
I'll help him. Can we pray?" Her tale's the tip
of icebergs: terrors, tears. We pray for peace.

ROOM 12

He's kindly, white-haired, greets me with a smile,
seems healthy. "Yes, I'm waiting to go home.
I had some trouble breathing for a while,
but now I'm fine. I like your job. That's some-
thing I did, too, for years. I'm old, you know:
a hundred years last month." "I wouldn't guess
a day past seventy!" He laughs. "Just so!
My calling kept me young, the work of bless-
ing people, loving them and God. But you
do that. You know." "I'm just a volunteer."
"That doesn't matter! So was Jesus. Do
you love the work?" I nod. "And did I hear
a code?" I nod. "He died. But anyway—"
"My dear." He reaches for my hand. "Let's pray."

ROOM 13

We have no thirteenth room; some patients might
fear even more misfortune. Being here's
bad luck aplenty, other numbers fright-
ening enough: pulse in the stratosphere,
high pressure, fever, labs mysterious
to all but the anointed, hieroglyphs
revealing failing organs, boisterous
infections, tumors. There are always ifs
in medicine, along with ands and buts;
all bets need hedging, even when the scopes
and scans seem black and white. But surgeons' cuts
are unequivocal, whatever hopes
their findings raise. With fear so overfed,
we don't make room for superstitious dread.

ROOM 14

Bed 14.1

One leg's a stump: the other's bloated, white,
looks ghastly. "Diabetes," he explains.
"They'll amputate tomorrow, but tonight
would suit me fine. I just can't take this pain!
They cut the first leg off five months ago;
I don't miss that one, either." But his wife
looks stricken, grieving. "Diabetes stinks,"
I tell them. Heartfelt nods. "What will your life
be like after the surgery?" He winks
and grins. "Oh, I'll be walking, have no fear!
A walker, two prostheses: I won't use
a wheelchair." "Good for you!" I'm both sincere
and slightly skeptical. "But don't refuse
to mourn. You've lost both legs: that's huge." His face
grows sad. "I know. Some things can't be replaced."

Bed 14.2

The boy has bruises, scrapes, eyes swollen shut
by injuries. His mother sits beside
the bed and holds his hand. "I don't know what
to do! The cops won't get involved. I tried
to tell them what he's up against: a gang,
five kids who beat him up because he's black.
They're Tongan. But the cops say, 'Kids' shenan-
igans,' because they're only twelve. I'd pack
and move, but money's tight. I told the school
we're way past bullying. They need to know:
he's facing outright violence! But the rule
appears to be, 'Ignore it till they go
to knives and guns.' He's scared, and so am I.
The doctor says he almost lost an eye."

Bed 14.3

His nasogastric tube is full of blood.
He moans in pain. The rotten reek of shit
surrounds the bed. "I know I don't smell good;
I'm sorry!" "Don't be, please; we're used to it!
You're in the hospital, and funky smells
come with the territory." *And gangrene's
much worse, believe me.* GI bleeds are hell
on every sense. He whimpers now, a keen-
ing howl. "Oh God, it hurts! Why won't they bring
my medicine?" I'd offer to go check,
except he's grabbed my hand. Abandoning
him now might seem like God disdains the wreck-
age of his works, avoids bad smells. I'll stay,
because God loves us always, any way.

WAITING ROOM

I always save the waiting room for last
to keep from duplicating visits back
in the department proper. There's no lack
of people: pacing, moaning, bored, harassed
by cranky kids—or frantic about kids
who lie too limply, drooping, somnolent.
I'm mostly here to field complaints: "They sent
in that guy, and my pain is worse than his!"
"They've taken folks who got here after us!"
"They're seeing people who aren't half as sick
as Mom!" "I know that being here's no fun;
I know this process seems mysterious.
But we're not trained to judge; the nurses pick
the sickest, truly." Triage 101.

FAST TRACK

I'm told that we can't call it "Urgent Care"
for billing reasons, but by any name
this is the place for minor ills: for sprains
and splinters, coughs and cuts, the wear and tear
of daily life. I try to stop here two
or three times in a shift; it's quiet, and
the staff's relaxed. We chat, swap weekend plans,
make jokes. But even here, some patients do
want prayer, need comfort. Take the widower,
the diabetic tourist who forgot
his insulin. "My wife's the one who packed,
who checked the lists, and after losing her,
I'm losing everything—my mind!" "You're not;
it's normal. Grief leaves no routine intact."

SIGNING OUT

Rewind, now: Wipe the "Susan" off the board
behind the nurse's station. Go upstairs
to document your hours and record
your visit tally, two dull digits where
the form says "Total," life and death reduced
to neat statistics, all that flesh and blood
erased. God's in the details, grace deduced
from tone and timing, story understood
as sacrament. Remove your badge; retrieve
your coat. Talk to yourself as you'd address
a child, instructing: *This is how we leave.*
It's nine o'clock. All edges coalesce,
blurred by fatigue. I only came at five,
and yet it feels like years since I arrived.

RETURNING HOME

The streets scroll by, deserted, as I steer
the car. I'm sluggish, grateful I live close
enough to get home quickly. Puppet shows
repeat behind my eyes, my own severe
reviews of what I should have done and said,
unkind post-mortem. I've grown to expect
this ruckus, conscience racing to inspect
each incident. To pry them from my head,
I turn the volume up on bouncy pop—
the Go-Go's—drive on autopilot, stay
the course. And here are house, cats, husband: zen
oasis. "Someone died," I say, and stop
as Gary hugs me. Sleep is far away;
and yet, next week, I'll do it all again.